MW00942817

the
junior chef
learning to cook step-by-step

Cypress Jones

Women's Weekly
THE AUSTRALIAN

CONTENTS

techniques 4

savoury 6

sweet 59

glossary 74

conversion chart 77

index 78

AUSTRALIAN CUP AND SPOON MEASUREMENTS ARE METRIC. A CONVERSION CHART APPEARS ON PAGE 77.

The cooking shows on television are having a positive effect on our kids – getting them into the kitchen. When kids cook, they are more likely to try new foods. Children need a hand when starting out, and the helpful step-by-step pictures in this book show how the recipes are made, teaching kids skills that will last them a lifetime.

Pamela Clark

Food Director

SEPARATING EGGS

Use the back of a butter knife to gently crack the egg over a small bowl. Transfer the yolk from half-shell to half-shell, being careful not to break the yolk, until all the egg white drops into the bowl. Place the yolk in another small bowl. Another way to do this is to carefully crack the egg into the cupped palm of your clean hand. Hold your hand over a small bowl with your fingers barely spread apart and let the egg white drop into the bowl while the yolk remains in your hand.

PEELING AND CRUSHING GARLIC

Separate garlic cloves from the bulb but do not peel; place on a chopping board then use the flat side of a heavy knife to press down firmly on each clove. As the clove is flattened, the skin splits and will be easy to pull off. Next, crush the garlic using a garlic press (pictured) or chop the garlic as the recipe says.

PEELING AND CHOPPING ONION

Cut the top end (not the root end) from the onion then cut it in half lengthways through the root end; peel and throw away the skin from both halves. To chop the onion finely (brunoise), slice each half thinly lengthways, without cutting all the way through to the root end; slice the onion thinly widthways, to give you small pieces or cubes of onion. To slice the onion thinly cut each half into thin slices widthways.

TECHNIQUES

FINELY GRATING CITRUS RIND

Use a microplane (pictured), the smallest holes on a grater, or a zester. Keep your fingers and knuckles out of the way and carefully grate the rind onto a piece of baking paper; it will slide easily off the paper. Don't press down too hard on the fruit – you only want to grate the outer coloured rind not the white pith underneath as it is bitter. If you need to juice the citrus fruit as well, always grate the rind first.

TURNING OUT A COOKED CAKE

Using oven mitts, or a thick dry tea towel, remove the cake pan from the oven and sit it on a heatproof mat or wooden board. Push a metal or wooden skewer into the cake then pull it out. If there is no cake mixture stuck to the skewer, the cake is cooked. Turn the cake pan upside-down onto a wire rack; remove the pan then the lining paper. Put another rack over the bottom of the cake and, holding the two racks like a sandwich, turn the cake over so it's top-side up.

SEPARATING LETTUCE LEAVES

Use a small knife to cut out the white core from the base of the lettuce. With the cored-end facing down, smash the lettuce hard onto the board – this loosens the outer leaves, which makes them come away easily in one piece (holding the cored-end under cold running water will also do this). Removing leaves this way is perfect for recipes like sang choy bow (page 55), which is served in lettuce cups. Separate leaves this way to chop or tear into bite-sized pieces.

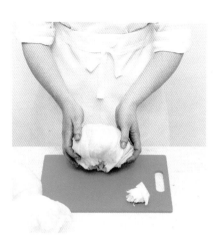

BOILED EGG WITH TOAST SOLDIERS

prep + cook time **30 minutes** serves **4**
nutritional count per serving 25.1g total fat
(11.7g saturated fat); 1994kJ (477 cal);
40.7g carbohydrate; 21g protein; 2.6g fibre

8 eggs
8 slices white bread (360g)
60g (2 ounces) butter, softened

1 Turn the stove on to high heat. Put the whole eggs into a medium saucepan; add enough cold water to cover the eggs. Put the saucepan on the heat; use a wooden spoon to stir the water constantly until it boils. This will ensure that the yolks are in the centre of the eggs when they are cooked.
2 Allow the water to continue boiling, without a lid, until the eggs are cooked the way you like them. As a guide, 3 minutes will give you set egg white and a soft yolk. After 5 minutes the yolk will be set as well (hard-boiled eggs).
3 Meanwhile, toast the bread, then spread it with the softened butter. Using a bread knife, cut the crusts off the toast, then cut each toast slice into four strips ("soldiers").
4 Empty the hot water out of the saucepan into the sink, being careful not to crack the eggs; hold the saucepan under cold running water for about 1 minute or until the eggs are cool enough to hold. This will stop a dark ring forming around the yolks. Serve the eggs in egg cups with toast "soldiers".

Cover the eggs with water in a saucepan. Stir constantly, over high heat, until the water boils.

Use a bread knife to cut the crusts off the buttered toast. Cut each slice of toast into four "soldiers."

Use a butter or small serrated knife to cut the tops off the boiled eggs so you can dip the toast into the yolks.

COOKED ENGLISH BREAKFAST

prep + cook time **20 minutes** serves **4**
nutritional count per serving **47.7g total fat**
(20.2g saturated fat); 2424kJ (580 cal);
3.5g carbohydrate; 34.6g protein; 2.4g fibre

50g (1½ ounces) butter
300g (9½ ounces) button mushrooms,
  cut in half
1 tablespoon vegetable oil
8 chipolata sausages (240g)
4 rindless bacon slices (260g)
2 medium tomatoes (300g), cut in half
8 eggs

1 Put the butter in a medium saucepan. Turn the stove on to medium heat and melt the butter. Add the mushrooms; stir with a wooden spoon for about 5 minutes or until they are tender. Take the saucepan off the heat; cover with a lid to keep the mushrooms warm.
2 Put half the oil in a large frying pan. Turn the stove on to medium heat and heat the pan. Add the sausages and bacon; cook them until the sausages are brown all over and cooked through and the bacon is crisp. Take the sausages and bacon out of the pan; put them on a plate. Cover with foil to keep them warm.

3 Turn on the grill (broiler) and let it heat up. Place the tomatoes, with cut sides up, on an oiled oven tray. Put the tray under the grill and cook the tomatoes until they start to soften.
4 Meanwhile, put the rest of the oil into the same large frying pan; turn the stove on to medium heat and heat the pan. Break an egg into a small bowl or cup, then carefully slide it into the hot oil; do this with three more eggs. Cook the eggs until they are done the way you like them. Use an egg slide to lift the eggs out of the pan; put them on four serving plates.
5 Repeat step 4 with the rest of the eggs (each person gets two eggs each). Spoon the mushrooms onto the plates. Use tongs to put the sausages, bacon and tomatoes onto the plates. Serve with toast.

tip **We used beef chipolata sausages, which are also known as "little fingers". They are spicy, coarse-textured sausages. You can use chicken or pork chipolatas or any sausages you like for this recipe.**

Cook the mushrooms in a medium saucepan until they are browned lightly and tender.

Place the tomatoes, cut-side up, onto an oiled oven tray. Place under a hot grill until softened.

Break the eggs, one at a time, into a small bowl, then carefully slide them into the hot frying pan.

PASSIONFRUIT SPARKLER

prep time **20 minutes (+ freezing)** makes **1 litre (4 cups)**
nutritional count per 1 cup (250ml) **0.5g total fat**
(0g saturated fat); 723kJ (173 cal); 31.1g carbohydrate;
4.1g protein; 13.2g fibre

340g (11 ounces) canned passionfruit in syrup
1 medium orange (240g)
150g (4½ ounces) seedless red grapes,
cut in half
1½ cups (375ml) pineapple juice, chilled
1½ cups (375ml) orange juice, chilled
1 cup (250ml) sparkling mineral water, chilled

1 Pour the passionfruit in syrup into a small jug, then pour it into ice-cube trays; place them in the freezer until frozen.
2 Peel the orange. Cut the orange into segments.
3 Put the frozen passionfruit cubes into a large jug with the orange segments and the rest of the ingredients; stir the drink gently to mix the ingredients together.

tip You can use any of your favourite fruits or fruit juices in this recipe.

Pour the passionfruit in syrup into a small jug. Carefully pour the passionfruit into ice-cube trays.

Run a small knife around the side of the orange to cut away the peel and the white pith.

To form wedges or segments, cut down the side of each membrane towards the centre of the orange.

NOODLE AND VEGETABLE RICE PAPER ROLLS

prep + cook time **40 minutes** makes **12**
nutritional count per roll **0.2g total fat (0g saturated fat);**
130kJ (31 cal); 6g carbohydrate; 1.1g protein; 0.6g fibre

60g (2 ounces) rice vermicelli noodles
1 small carrot (70g), grated coarsely
200g (6½ ounces) wombok (napa cabbage),
   shredded finely
1 tablespoon fish sauce
1 tablespoon light brown sugar
¼ cup (60ml) lemon juice
12 x 17cm (6¾-inch) square rice paper sheets
12 fresh mint leaves

1 Put the noodles in a medium heatproof bowl. Pour in enough boiling water to cover the noodles; leave them until they are tender. Pour the noodles into a colander or sieve over the sink and drain off the water. Use a pair of kitchen scissors to cut the noodles into different lengths.
2 Clean the bowl from step 1; put the noodles back into the bowl. Add the carrot, cabbage, fish sauce, sugar and lemon juice to the bowl; use tongs to mix the ingredients together.

3 Put one sheet of rice paper into a medium bowl of warm water; leave until it is just soft. Lift the sheet from the water carefully; put it on a board covered with a clean tea towel, with a corner of the rice paper sheet pointing towards you.
4 Put a rounded tablespoon of the vegetable filling mixture horizontally across the lower part of the rice paper sheet; put one mint leaf on top. Hold the corner of the sheet facing you; fold it over the filling. Roll the sheet to cover the filling, then fold in the sides. Continue rolling the sheet to enclose the filling. Do this with the rest of the rice paper sheets, filling mixture and mint leaves.

tips Serve the rice paper rolls with a mild sweet chilli sauce or soy sauce for dipping.
The rolls can be made ahead of time and stored in the fridge for up to 3 hours. Cover them with a damp clean tea towel to keep them moist.
The rice paper sheets are very fragile, so handle them gently as they can tear once moistened.

Lift the soft rice paper sheet from the water; put it on a clean tea towel, with a corner of the sheet pointing towards you.

Place the filling horizontally across the lower part of the rice paper sheet; put one mint leaf on top. Fold the corner over filling.

Fold in both sides then continue to roll forward to completely enclose the filling. Be careful, as the rice paper may tear.

CHICKEN, MAYO, CELERY AND WALNUT SANDWICHES

prep time 35 minutes   makes 30 triangles
nutritional count per triangle 6.6g total fat
(1.5g saturated fat); 752kJ (180 cal);
20.4g carbohydrate; 8.5g protein; 2.1g fibre

3 cups (480g) finely chopped cooked chicken
4 green onions (scallions), chopped finely
½ cup (60g) finely chopped roasted walnuts
3 stalks celery (450g), with leafy ends cut off,
    and the stalk chopped finely
½ cup (150g) mayonnaise
⅓ cup (80g) sour cream
20 slices white bread (900g)
10 slices wholemeal bread (450g)

1 Put the chicken, onion, walnuts, celery, mayonnaise and sour cream into a large bowl; mix the ingredients together with a spoon.
2 Spread half the chicken mixture over 10 slices of white bread; put a slice of wholemeal bread on top of each. Spread the rest of the chicken mixture over the wholemeal bread; put the other 10 white bread slices on top.
3 Use a serrated bread knife to cut the crusts off the sandwiches; cut each sandwich into four triangles.

tip To save time chopping the walnuts, put the roasted nuts in a food processor and pulse a few times until the nuts are finely chopped but not ground.

Spread half the chicken mixture over 10 slices of white bread. Top each with a slice of wholemeal bread.

Spread with the rest of the chicken mixture over the top of the bread, then top with remaining bread.

Use a bread knife to cut the crusts off the sandwiches, then cut each sandwich into four triangles.

CLUB SANDWICH

prep + cook time **25 minutes** makes **4**
nutritional count per sandwich **36.1g total fat**
(7.7g saturated fat); 3210kJ (768 cal);
69.9g carbohydrate; 37.7g protein; 6.3g fibre

4 rindless bacon slices (260g), cut in half
1 medium avocado (250g), cut in half and
    seed removed
2 teaspoons lime juice
½ cup (150g) mayonnaise
12 slices white bread (540g)
12 large butter (boston) lettuce leaves, discard
    the white parts, and roughly tear the leaves
3 small tomatoes (270g), sliced thinly
150g (4½ ounces) shaved turkey breast

1 Put a large frying pan on the stove and turn
the heat on to high. Put the bacon in the pan;
cook until crisp, using tongs to turn it over.
Take the bacon out of the pan and put on a
plate covered with absorbent paper.
2 Put the avocado and lime juice in a small
bowl; mash the avocado mixture with the back
of a fork until smooth.

3 Spread the mayonnaise over one side of the
bread slices. Take four slices of bread and
spread them with half the avocado; top with
half the lettuce, tomato, turkey and bacon. Put
one slice of bread, mayonnaise-side down, on
top of each sandwich; spread the top-side of
the bread with a little more mayonnaise, then
the rest of the avocado mixture. Top with the
rest of the lettuce, tomato, turkey and bacon;
place the last four slices of bread, mayonnaise-
side down, on top of the fillings.
4 Stick skewers through the sandwiches to
keep the layers of filling in place. Use a serrated
bread knife to cut the sandwiches in half.

tips We made our club sandwich with fresh white bread,
but you can toast the bread first if you like.
To save washing up, cook the bacon in the microwave.
Put it on a plate lined with a piece of absorbent paper
then cook it on HIGH (100%) for 1-2 minutes or until
browned and crisp.

Use a small knife to carefully cut the
avocado in half, around the seed;
scoop the seed out with a spoon.

Spread the bread with avocado; top
with lettuce, tomato, turkey and
bacon, then another slice of bread.

Repeat the layer to make a
double-decker sandwich. Skewer
the sandwich, then cut it in half.

BRUSCHETTA FINGERS

prep + cook time **20 minutes** serves **8**
nutritional count per serving **6.4g total fat**
(2.2g saturated fat); 903kJ (216 cal);
29.9g carbohydrate; 8.2g protein; 2.7g fibre

4 small turkish bread rolls (440g)
2 tablespoons sun-dried tomato pesto
250g (8 ounces) cherry tomatoes, cut into
  quarters
120g (4 ounces) baby bocconcini cheese,
  sliced thinly
2 tablespoons finely chopped fresh
  flat-leaf parsley

1 Turn on the grill (broiler) and let it heat up.
2 Cut the bread rolls in half and put them,
cut-sides up, on an oven tray. Put the tray
under the grill and toast the bread rolls until
they are light brown. Take the tray from under
the grill and put the bread rolls on a board.
Using a bread knife, cut the bread rolls into
2cm (¾-inch) wide strips ("fingers").
3 Spread the toasted sides of the bread with
pesto; top with tomato and cheese. Place the
bruschetta fingers on a plate; sprinkle with
parsley just before serving.

Use a bread knife to cut the toasted
rolls into 2cm (¾-inch) wide strips
("fingers").

Spread the toasted sides with
pesto; put the tomato and cheese
on top, then sprinkle with parsley.

MINI CABANOSSI PIZZAS

prep + cook time **25 minutes** makes **12**
nutritional count per pizza **5.1g total fat**
(2.1g saturated fat); 644kJ (154 cal);
19.6g carbohydrate; 6.5g protein; 1.5g fibre

1 small zucchini (90g)
440g (14-ounce) pizza base with tomato sauce
100g (3 ounces) cabanossi, sliced thinly
12 cherry bocconcini cheese (130g), cut in half

1 Turn the oven on to 220°C/425°F and let it heat up. Use baking paper to line an oven tray.
2 Coarsely grate the zucchini; put zucchini in a fine sieve over the sink or a small bowl, then use clean hands to squeeze out any excess liquid.
3 Use a 6.5cm (2½-inch) fluted round cutter to cut 12 rounds from the pizza base; put the rounds on the oven tray.
4 Put cabanossi, zucchini and two pieces of cheese on top of each round. Cook pizzas in the oven for about 10 minutes or until they are heated through. Serve warm or cold.

tips You can buy prepared pizza bases from the supermarket; they can be found in the refrigerated, freezer or bakery sections.
Zucchini have a lot of water in them; squeezing the water out of the grated zucchini prevents the pizza bases getting soggy.

Put the grated zucchini in a fine sieve over a small bowl; press to remove as much liquid as possible.

Use a 6.5cm (2½-inch) fluted round cutter to cut 12 rounds from the pizza base.

Put pizza rounds on a lined oven tray; top with cabanossi, zucchini and two pieces of cheese.

TOMATO, FETTA AND BACON FRITTATAS

prep + cook time **40 minutes** makes **6**
nutritional count per frittata 24.4g total fat
(13.4g saturated fat); 1216kJ (291 cal);
1.6g carbohydrate; 17g protein; 0.4g fibre

2 rindless bacon slices (130g), chopped
   coarsely
100g (3 ounces) fetta cheese, broken into
   small pieces
¼ cup (20g) finely grated parmesan cheese
⅓ cup coarsely chopped fresh basil
6 eggs
⅔ cup (160ml) pouring cream
9 baby egg (plum) tomatoes (150g), cut in
   half lengthways

1 Turn the oven on to 180°C/350°F and let it
heat up. Use a little cooking-oil spray to grease
a 6-hole (¾-cup/180ml) texas muffin pan. Using
a small bowl or the muffin pan as a guide, cut
six circles of baking paper just large enough to
line the base of each pan hole.
2 Divide bacon, fetta, parmesan and basil
between pan holes. Break eggs, one at a time,
into a small bowl, then pour into a large jug.
When all the eggs are in the jug, beat them well
with a whisk. Add the cream and whisk it into
the eggs. Pour the egg mixture into the pan holes.
Put three tomato halves on top of each frittata.
3 Put the muffin pan in the oven and bake the
frittatas for about 25 minutes. Take the pan out
of the oven; leave it for 5 minutes. Use a palette
knife to loosen the edges of the frittatas before
carefully turning them out onto a board. Remove
the baking paper from the bases of the frittatas
before serving.

tips Lining the base of each pan hole with baking paper
makes it easier to get the cooked frittatas out. Using a
pencil, trace circles around the base of the pan or a
small bowl (the same size as the pan holes) onto baking
paper, then cut them out with scissors. Place the circles
into the pan holes, making sure the sides with the pencil
marks are facing down.

Using a small bowl or base of the
muffin pan as a guide, trace six
circles onto baking paper, no larger
than the base of the pan holes.

Divide bacon, cheeses and basil
between the lined pan holes, then
carefully pour in the egg mixture.

Use a palette knife to loosen the
edges of the cooked frittatas before
turning them out of the pan.

BEAN AND CORIANDER QUESADILLAS

prep + cook time **20 minutes** serves **4**
nutritional count per serving **15g total fat**
(8.4g saturated fat); 1898kJ (454 cal);
49.5g carbohydrate; 23.3g protein; 13.4g fibre

840g (1¾ pounds) canned mexe-beans, with
liquid drained off, mashed with a fork
16 mini (15cm/6-inch) flour tortillas (400g)
2 large tomatoes (440g), seeds removed,
chopped finely
½ cup coarsely chopped fresh coriander
(cilantro)
1½ cups (180g) coarsely grated cheddar
cheese

1 Turn on the sandwich press and let it heat up.
2 Spread the mashed beans over eight of the
tortillas; sprinkle them with tomato, coriander
and cheese. Put the other eight tortillas on top.
3 Put the quesadillas into the sandwich press;
cook until they are browned on both sides and
heated through.
4 Cut quesadillas into wedges to serve.

serving idea **Serve quesadillas with sour cream,**
sliced avocado and lime wedges.
tip **If you don't have a sandwich press you can cook**
the quesadillas under a preheated grill (broiler), turning
once, until they are browned both sides and crisp.

Cut the tomatoes in half then use a
teaspoon to scoop out the seeds.

Spread mashed beans over half the
tortillas; top with tomato, coriander,
cheese then the remaining tortillas.

SPINACH, HAM AND POACHED EGG ON TOAST

prep + cook time **20 minutes** serves **4**
nutritional count per serving **9.5g total fat**
(2.6g saturated fat); 1371kJ (328 cal);
37.3g carbohydrate; 21.5g protein; 2.9g fibre

4 eggs
2 turkish bread rolls (330g)
75g (2½ ounces) baby spinach leaves
150g (4½ ounces) shaved ham

1 Half-fill a large frying pan with water. Turn the
stove on to high and boil the water. Break one
egg into a small bowl or cup, then slide the egg
into the pan of boiling water, being careful not
to break the yolk. Do this, one at a time, with
the rest of the eggs. When all the eggs are in
the pan, allow the water to boil again. Put a
lid on the pan, and turn off the heat; leave for
about 4 minutes or until the yolks are covered
with a light film of set egg white.
2 Meanwhile, cut each roll in half horizontally so
you have two thick slices; toast the cut sides
under a preheated grill (broiler). Top toasted
sides with spinach and ham.

3 Place a piece of absorbent paper on a plate.
Use a slotted spoon to lift one egg out of the
water, resting the spoon on the paper to soak
up the poaching liquid. Do this, one at a time,
with the rest of the eggs.
4 Place the eggs on top of the ham; serve
immediately.

tips **Fresh eggs have thicker whites and will hold a neat
shape when poaching. If your poached eggs look a little
untidy, place the drained eggs on a chopping board and
use a small knife to trim the edges of the whites.**

Break one egg into a small bowl,
then carefully slide the egg into
the pan of boiling water.

Use a slotted spoon to lift cooked
eggs from the pan. Rest the spoon on
absorbent paper to soak up liquid.

BACON AND POTATO SOUP

prep + cook time **45 minutes** serves **6**
nutritional count per serving **26.4g total fat**
(15.5g saturated fat); 1747kJ (418 cal);
24.1g carbohydrate; 20g protein; 3g fibre

**6 rindless bacon slices (390g), chopped
  coarsely**
4 cloves garlic, crushed
2 cups (500ml) water
**1kg (2 pounds) potatoes, peeled and
  chopped coarsely**
1 cup (250ml) chicken stock
1¼ cups (300g) sour cream
¼ cup finely chopped fresh flat-leaf parsley

1 Put a little oil in a large saucepan. Turn the
stove on to medium heat and heat the pan.
Add the bacon and garlic to the pan; stir with
a wooden spoon until the bacon is crisp.
2 Add the water, potato and stock; turn up the
heat to high and boil the soup. Turn down the
heat. Put a lid on the saucepan; let the soup
simmer for about 10 minutes or until the potato
is tender. Add the sour cream to the soup; stir
until the cream is just heated through (do not
let it boil or the soup may curdle). Take the
saucepan off the stove. Stir in the parsley. Serve
the soup topped with extra parsley leaves.

tips You can buy chicken stock in tetra packs from
the supermarket.
For information about how to peel and crush garlic
see page 4.

Cook the bacon and garlic, stirring
with a wooden spoon, until the
bacon is browned and crisp.

Once the potato is tender, stir the
sour cream into the soup until it is
just heated through; do not boil.

PEA AND HAM SOUP

prep + cook time **2 hours 15 minutes** serves **6**
nutritional count per serving **4.9g total fat**
(1.4g saturated fat); 1162kJ (278 cal);
31g carbohydrate; 23.5g protein; 7.3g fibre

1 medium brown onion (150g), peeled and
    chopped coarsely
2 stalks celery (300g), leafy ends discarded,
    and stalks chopped coarsely
2 dried bay leaves
1.5kg (3 pounds) ham hocks
2.5 litres (10 cups) water
1 teaspoon cracked black pepper
2 cups (375g) split green peas

1 Put the onion, celery, bay leaves, ham hocks,
water and pepper into a large saucepan. Turn
the stove on to high heat and boil the soup.
Turn down the heat. Put a lid on the saucepan
and let the soup simmer for about 1½ hours.
2 Add the peas to the soup. Put the lid back on
and let the soup simmer for about 30 minutes
or until the peas are tender.
3 Take the saucepan off the stove; place on
a heatproof mat on the bench. Use tongs to
carefully lift the ham hocks out of the saucepan;
put them into a heatproof bowl. When they are
cool enough to touch, remove the meat from
the bones with clean hands; shred the meat

finely with a fork. Throw away the bones, fat and
skin. Use a slotted spoon to remove the bay
leaves from the soup and throw them away.
4 Take about half the soup mixture out of the
saucepan; place it in a large jug or bowl. Pour
small amounts of this mixture into a blender or
food processor; blend or process until smooth.
Do this in batches until you have blended all the
mixture in the jug. Pour the blended mixture
back into the saucepan with the rest of the
soup mixture. Add the ham meat; stir the soup
until it has heated through.

tips Split peas don't need to be soaked in water overnight,
however, give them a rinse under cold water to remove
any grit. The relatively short cooking time for the peas
produces a soup with more texture.
For information about how to peel and chop onion see
page 4.

Use tongs to carefully remove the
ham hocks from the soup and put
them into a heatproof bowl.

Remove the meat from the ham
bones and place it on a board.
Use a fork to shred the meat finely.

Carefully pour the blended soup
mixture back into the pan with the
rest of the soup and shredded ham.

POTATO WEDGES WITH GUACAMOLE

prep + cook time **1 hour** serves **4**
nutritional count per serving **34.9g total fat**
(7.1g saturated fat); 1952kJ (467 cal);
27.9g carbohydrate; 7.6g protein; 6.3g fibre

4 medium potatoes (800g), unpeeled
1 tablespoon olive oil
1 tablespoon chicken seasoning
cooking-oil spray
guacamole
3 medium avocados (750g), cut in half and
    seeds removed
½ small red onion (50g), peeled and
    chopped finely
1 small egg (plum) tomato (60g), seeds
    removed and chopped finely
1 tablespoon lime juice
¼ cup coarsely chopped fresh coriander
    (cilantro)

1 Turn on the oven to 240°C/475°F and let it heat up.
2 Wash and scrub the potatoes well to remove any dirt from the skins; pat them dry with absorbent kitchen paper.

3 Cut the potatoes in half; cut each half into wedges. Put the wedges into a medium bowl with the oil and chicken seasoning; turn the wedges with tongs so they are covered all over with the oil mixture.
4 Lightly spray a large baking dish with cooking oil. Put the wedges in the dish then put the dish in the oven. Bake about 40 minutes or until the wedges are golden brown.
5 Make guacamole (see recipe below). Serve wedges with guacamole.
guacamole Scoop the avocado flesh out of each half with a spoon and put it in a medium bowl; mash with the back of a fork. Stir in the onion, tomato, lime juice and coriander. (Makes 2½ cups).

tips **If your potatoes are really dirty you can use a soft**
scrubbing brush to help get the dirt off.
For information about how to remove the seeds from
avocados see page 16.
For information about how to peel and chop onion see
page 4.

Wash and scrub any dirt off the potatoes then pat them dry with some absorbent kitchen paper.

Cut each potato in half then cut each half into four wedges. Combine the wedges, oil and seasoning.

Cut the tomato in half then use a teaspoon to scoop out the seeds from each tomato half.

CREAMED CORN AND BACON STUFFED POTATOES

prep + cook time **45 minutes** serves **4**

nutritional count per serving **2g total fat**

(0.3g saturated fat); 878kJ (210 cal);

36.7g carbohydrate; 7.8g protein; 5.9g fibre

8 coliban potatoes (960g), unpeeled
1 teaspoon vegetable oil
1 rindless bacon slice (65g), chopped
    coarsely
125g (4 ounces) canned creamed corn
2 tablespoons finely chopped fresh
    coriander (cilantro)

1 Turn on the oven to 200°C/400°F and let it heat up. Spray an oven tray with a little cooking oil, then cover the tray with baking paper.

2 Cook the potatoes by boiling, steaming or microwaving them until they are just tender. Pour the potatoes into a colander over the sink and drain off the liquid.

3 Meanwhile, put the oil into a small frying pan. Turn the stove on to medium heat and heat the pan. Add the bacon to the pan; stir with a wooden spoon for about 2 minutes or until it is crisp. Turn off the heat.

4 Cut a shallow slice, about 1cm (½ inch), from the top of each potato. Use a teaspoon to scoop the flesh out of the potato tops; put the flesh into a medium bowl, throw away the skins from the potato tops.

5 Carefully scoop about two-thirds of the flesh from each potato base; put the flesh into the bowl. Keep the potato "shells".

6 Use a potato masher to mash the potato flesh in the bowl until it is smooth. Add the bacon, corn and coriander; stir them into the mashed potato.

7 Place the potato shells onto the lined oven tray. Spoon the mashed potato mixture into the potato shells. Put the tray in the oven and bake for about 15 minutes or until the potato is heated through.

tips We used coliban potatoes (often sold as washed potatoes in the supermarket) because they have very fine skins that are pleasant to eat.

If you don't like coriander, you can use the same amount of flat-leaf parsley instead.

Cut a small slice from the top of the potatoes. Use a teaspoon to scoop the flesh from the tops into a bowl.

Use a teaspoon to scoop two-thirds of the flesh from each potato into the bowl to make potato "shells."

Place the shells on a lined oven tray. Spoon the mashed potato and corn mixture into the potato shells.

BLT SALAD

prep + cook time 35 minutes serves 4
nutritional count per serving 31.2g total fat
(16.4g saturated fat); 2312kJ (553 cal);
31.1g carbohydrate; 33.9g protein; 7.1g fibre

250g (8 ounces) cherry tomatoes
cooking-oil spray
6 rindless bacon slices (390g)
1 small french bread stick (150g)
180g (5½ ounces) bocconcini cheese,
    cut into chunks
1 large cos lettuce, with leaves separated
    and torn up
mustard mayonnaise
⅓ cup (100g) mayonnaise
¼ cup (60ml) lemon juice
2 teaspoons wholegrain mustard

1 Turn on the grill (broiler) and let it heat up.

2 Make the mustard mayonnaise (see recipe below).

3 Put the tomatoes on an oven tray; spray them with cooking oil. Put the bacon on the same tray. Cook under the grill until the tomatoes are slightly soft and the bacon is browned and crisp. Take the tray from under the grill; use tongs to lift the bacon onto absorbent paper. When the bacon is cool enough to touch, chop it coarsely. Cover the tomatoes and bacon with foil to keep them warm.

4 Use a bread knife to cut the bread into eight slices; put the slices under the grill to toast on both sides.

5 Put the tomato, bacon, cheese and lettuce into a large bowl; mix them together with tongs. Divide the salad between four serving dishes. Pour the mustard mayonnaise over the salad; serve with toast.

mustard mayonnaise Mix the ingredients in a small bowl with a spoon.

tip For information about how to separate lettuce leaves see page 5.

Drain the cooked, crisp bacon on absorbent paper then cut it into chunks on a chopping board.

Use a bread knife to cut the bread stick into eight slices.

GREEK SALAD

prep time **20 minutes** serves **4**
nutritional count per serving **25.8g total fat**
(9.6g saturated fat); 1359kJ (325 cal);
10.8g carbohydrate; 11.5g protein; 3.2g fibre

¼ cup (60ml) olive oil
1 tablespoon lemon juice
1 tablespoon white wine vinegar
1 tablespoon finely chopped fresh oregano
1 clove garlic, crushed
3 medium tomatoes (450g), cut into wedges
2 lebanese cucumbers (260g), chopped
   coarsely
1 small red onion (100g), peeled and
   sliced thinly
1 small red capsicum (bell pepper) (150g),
   sliced thinly
½ cup (75g) black olives without seeds
200g (6½ ounces) fetta cheese, chopped
   coarsely

1 Put the oil, lemon juice, vinegar, oregano and
garlic into a large bowl; beat them together
with a whisk.
2 Add the rest of the ingredients to the bowl;
use tongs or a large spoon to mix them
together gently.

tips Remove the core, seeds and membranes from the
capsicum before you cut it into thin slices.
For information about how to peel and slice an onion
and peel and crush garlic see page 4.

Cut top off capsicum; lift it off
pulling away the core and seeds.
Pull off any bits of white membrane.

Cut the tomatoes in half. Cut each
half into four wedges. Cut off any
bits of the hard grey stem.

VIETNAMESE BEEF SALAD

prep + cook time **40 minutes** (+ refrigeration) serves **4**
nutritional count per serving **19.4g total fat**
(4.1g saturated fat); 1371kJ (328 cal);
6.2g carbohydrate; 29.7g protein; 4.6g fibre

500g (1 pound) beef rump steak, sliced thinly
4 cloves garlic, crushed
2 teaspoons fish sauce
1 teaspoon caster (superfine) sugar
1 medium butter (boston) lettuce, with leaves
    separated and white parts cut off
250g (8 ounces) cherry tomatoes, cut in half
1 small red onion (100g), peeled and
    sliced thinly
½ telegraph cucumber (200g), chopped
    coarsely
1 cup loosely packed fresh mint leaves
1½ tablespoons rice vinegar
1 tablespoon olive oil
¼ cup (35g) coarsely chopped unsalted
    peanuts
1 tablespoon peanut oil

1 Put the beef, garlic, fish sauce and sugar in a medium bowl. Cover with plastic wrap; put the bowl in the fridge for 20 minutes.
2 Meanwhile, put the lettuce, tomato, onion, cucumber, mint, rice vinegar and olive oil in a large bowl.
3 Put a wok on the stove; turn the stove on to medium heat. Put the peanuts in the wok; stir them constantly with a wooden spoon until they are light brown. Use a large spoon to take the peanuts out of the hot wok; put them in a bowl.
4 Put the peanut oil in the wok. Turn the stove on to high heat and heat the wok. Add the beef, in batches; stir-fry each batch of beef until it is brown. Take each batch out of the wok and put it in a heatproof bowl before stir-frying the next batch.
5 Place the salad onto four serving plates. Top with the beef; sprinkle with the roasted peanuts.

tips You can use any type of lettuce you like.
For information about how to peel and slice onion and crush garlic see page 4.

Use a sharp knife to slice the beef
as thinly as you can.

Cook the nuts in a heated dry wok
until they are light brown.

Cook the beef, in batches, until
browned all over.

SPAGHETTI CARBONARA WITH PEAS

prep + cook time **25 minutes** serves **4**
nutritional count per serving **15.3g total fat**
(6.3g saturated fat); 2332kJ (558 cal);
66.8g carbohydrate; 35g protein; 5.1g fibre

4 egg yolks
¾ cup (60g) finely grated parmesan cheese
4 rindless bacon slices (260g), chopped finely
2 cloves garlic, sliced thinly
1 cup (120g) frozen peas
375g (12 ounces) spaghetti

1 Put the egg yolks and cheese into a small bowl; mix them together with a fork.
2 Put a medium frying pan on the stove and turn on the heat to medium-high. Add the bacon to the pan; stir with a wooden spoon for about 5 minutes or until the bacon is crisp. Add the garlic; stir for 1 minute. Add the peas; stir until they are heated through.

3 Meanwhile, fill a large saucepan with water. Turn the stove on to high heat and boil the water. Add the spaghetti; cook until it is tender (check the instructions on the packet for how long this should take). Remove and save ¼ cup of the cooking liquid, then drain the spaghetti into a colander. Put the spaghetti back into the saucepan.
4 Add the bacon mixture, egg mixture and the saved cooking liquid to the saucepan. Put the pan back on the stove and turn the heat to medium; stir with a wooden spoon or tongs for 1 minute to mix the spaghetti and sauce together.

tips For information about how to peel and slice garlic see page 4.
When adding the spaghetti to the saucepan of boiling water, fan it out with your hand to try and keep the strands of spaghetti separate so they won't stick together. Use a pair of tongs with a long handle to stir the spaghetti a few times while it is cooking – this will also help to stop the pasta sticking together.

Cook the bacon in a frying pan until crisp. Add the garlic to the pan and cook, stirring, for 1 minute.

Carefully add spaghetti to a pan of boiling water. Stir with a long pair of tongs to separate the spaghetti.

Stir the drained spaghetti, bacon mixture, egg mixture and cooking liquid over heat until mixed well.

HERB-CRUMBED LAMB RACKS

prep + cook time **35 minutes** serves **4**
nutritional count per serving **25g total fat**
(12.6g saturated fat); 1538kJ (368 cal);
13.7g carbohydrate; 21.4g protein; 1.9g fibre

cooking-oil spray
2 slices white bread (90g), crusts removed,
  bread torn into pieces
2 tablespoons fresh flat-leaf parsley leaves
¼ cup loosely packed fresh mint leaves
2 teaspoons finely grated lemon rind
40g (1½ ounces) butter
2 shallots (50g), peeled and chopped finely
4 x 4 french-trimmed lamb cutlet racks (720g)
250g (8 ounces) baby vine-ripened truss
  tomatoes

1 Turn on the oven to 200°C/400°F and let it
heat up. Spray the inside of a large baking dish
with cooking oil.
2 Put the bread, herbs and lemon rind in a
food processor; process until ingredients are
chopped finely. Put mixture into a small bowl.

3 Put the butter in a small frying pan. Turn the
stove on to medium heat and melt the butter.
Pour half the melted butter into the breadcrumb
mixture; mix it in with a wooden spoon.
4 Add the shallot to the rest of the melted
butter in the pan; stir with a wooden spoon,
over medium heat, until the shallot is soft.
Pour the shallot mixture into the breadcrumb
mixture; mix it in.
5 Put the lamb and tomatoes into the baking
dish; spray the tomatoes with cooking oil. Use
clean hands to press the breadcrumb mixture
firmly onto the lamb.
6 Put the dish in the oven and bake about
20 minutes or until the lamb is cooked the
way you like it. Serve the lamb with the
roasted tomatoes.

tip To judge whether the lamb is cooked the way you
like it, press the surface with your finger or the back of
a pair of tongs. Rare (red in the middle) feels soft and
spongy, medium-rare (pinkish-red in the middle) feels
soft but springy, medium (pink in the middle) feels firm
but still springy, and well-done (no pink left in the
middle) feels quite firm.

Pour half the melted butter into the
breadcrumb mixture and mix it in
well using a wooden spoon.

Add the shallot to the rest of the
melted butter in the pan; cook over
medium heat until the shallot is soft.

Use clean hands to press the
breadcrumb mixture firmly onto
the top side of the lamb racks.

MEATBALLS NAPOLETANA

prep + cook time **1 hour** serves **4**
nutritional count per serving **18.2g total fat**
(5.7g saturated fat); 1831kJ (438 cal);
30.5g carbohydrate; 35.3g protein; 5.4g fibre

500g (1 pound) minced (ground) pork and veal
1 egg
¼ cup (20g) finely grated parmesan cheese
½ cup (50g) packaged breadcrumbs
¼ cup finely chopped fresh flat-leaf parsley
1 tablespoon olive oil
1 small brown onion (80g), peeled and
   chopped finely
1 clove garlic, crushed
700g (1½ pounds) bottled tomato pasta sauce
½ cup (60g) frozen peas
¼ cup coarsely chopped fresh basil
½ cup (60g) green olives without seeds

1 Put the pork and veal mince, egg, cheese, breadcrumbs and parsley in a medium bowl; use clean hands to mix them together. Roll level tablespoons of the mince mixture into balls.

2 Put half the oil in a large frying pan. Turn the stove on to medium heat and heat the pan. Add the meatballs; cook the meatballs, turning them, until they are brown all over and cooked through. Use tongs to remove the meatballs from the pan into a medium heatproof bowl.
3 Put the rest of the oil into the frying pan. Turn the stove on to medium heat and heat the pan. Add the onion and garlic; stir with a wooden spoon until the onion is soft. Add the pasta sauce; turn the heat up and bring the mixture to the boil. Put the meatballs back into the pan, then turn down the heat; simmer, uncovered, for about 10 minutes or until the sauce thickens slightly.
4 Add the peas and basil to the pan, then simmer, uncovered, for about 2 minutes or until the peas are tender. Add the olives and stir until the olives are heated through.

tips Some butchers sell a pork and veal mixture, which is what we use here. If it is not available as a mixture, buy 250g (8 ounces) of pork mince and 250g (8 ounces) of veal mince.
For information about how to peel and slice an onion and peel and crush garlic see page 4.
serving idea Serve the meatballs and sauce with spaghetti. Cook about 375g (12 ounces) of dried spaghetti to make enough cooked spaghetti to serve four with this sauce.

Use clean hands to mix the pork and veal mince, egg, breadcrumbs, cheese and parsley together well.

Take level tablespoons of the mince mixture and roll it in your hands to form the meatballs.

Add the cooked meatballs to the sauce and simmer, uncovered, until the sauce thickens slightly.

CHICKEN AND VEGETABLE PASTIES

prep + cook time **50 minutes** makes **4**
nutritional count per pastie **62.5g total fat**
(32.3g saturated fat); 4063kJ (972 cal);
69.1g carbohydrate; 31.4g protein; 5.9g fibre

2 teaspoons vegetable oil
2 cloves garlic, crushed
1 medium brown onion (150g), peeled and
  chopped finely
1½ cups (240g) coarsely chopped barbecued
  chicken
2 cups (240g) frozen pea, corn and carrot
  mixture
2 teaspoons dijon mustard
½ cup (120g) sour cream
¼ cup (30g) coarsely grated cheddar cheese
4 sheets puff pastry
1 egg, beaten lightly

1 Turn on the oven to 220°C/425°F and let it
heat up. Spray an oven tray with cooking oil.
2 Put the oil in a large frying pan. Turn the
stove on to medium heat and heat the pan.
Add the garlic and onion; stir with a wooden
spoon until the onion is soft.

3 Add the chicken, frozen vegetables, mustard,
sour cream and cheese; stir the mixture until it
is heated all the way through.
4 Put the pastry sheets, one at a time, on a
board. Cut one 22cm (9-inch) round from each
pastry sheet (use a 22cm/9-inch plate or cake
pan as a guide). Place one quarter of the filling
in the centre of each round. Use a pastry brush
to brush the edge of the pastry with the egg.
Fold the pastry rounds in half to enclose the
filling; use your thumb and forefinger to pinch
the edges together to seal the pasties.
5 Place the pasties on the oven tray; use a
pastry brush to brush the tops with the rest
of the egg. Put the tray in the oven and bake
for about 30 minutes or until the pasties are
golden brown.

tips For information about how to peel and chop onion
and crush garlic see page 4.
You will need about half a large barbecued chicken for
this recipe.
Uncooked pasties can be frozen for up to three months.
Make the pasties up to the end of step 4. Put them in an
airtight container, between sheets of baking paper, and
freeze them. When you want to eat them, put them in
the fridge for a few hours to thaw, then bake.

Cut around a 22cm (9-inch) diameter
plate to get one round from each
sheet of pastry.

Spoon one-quarter of the chicken
and vegetable filling into the middle
of each pastry round.

Fold the pastry rounds in half to
enclose the filling. Pinch the pastry
edges together to seal.

CHICKEN FRIED RICE

prep + cook time **30 minutes** serves **4**

nutritional count per serving **21.9g total fat**
(5.9g saturated fat); 2362kJ (565 cal);
52.6g carbohydrate; 37.2g protein; 3.8g fibre

2 eggs, beaten lightly
1 tablespoon vegetable oil
3 rindless bacon slices (195g), chopped
    coarsely
2 cloves garlic, crushed
2cm (¾-inch) piece fresh ginger (10g), peeled
    and grated
1½ cups (240g) coarsely chopped cooked
    chicken
4 cups cold cooked rice (see tips)
1 cup (140g) frozen pea and corn mixture
¼ cup (60ml) light soy sauce
1 cup (80g) bean sprouts
6 green onions (scallions), sliced thinly

1 Break eggs, one at a time, into a small bowl,
then pour into a large jug. Beat the eggs with
a whisk until they are mixed well. Put half the
oil into a wok. Turn the stove on to medium
heat and heat the wok. Pour the eggs into the
wok; swirl the wok to spread the egg into a
thin omelette. Use an egg slide to slide the
omelette out of the wok onto a board. Leave
it to cool down. Roll up the omelette tightly,
then cut the roll into thin strips.
2 Put the rest of the oil into the wok and turn
the stove on to medium-high heat. Add the
bacon, garlic and ginger; stir with a wooden
spoon until the bacon is crisp.
3 Add the chicken; stir-fry for 1 minute. Add
the rice, frozen vegetables and soy sauce;
stir-fry until hot. Add the sprouts, onion and
omelette; stir-fry for 1 minute.

tips You will need to cook 1½ cups (300g) white
long-grain rice the day before you make this recipe.
Spread the cooked rice evenly onto a tray; leave it
uncovered and put it in the fridge overnight. This dries
out the rice so that the fried rice will not be gluggy.
For information about how to peel and crush garlic see
page 4.

Spread the cooked rice onto a tray;
leave it uncovered and put it in the
fridge overnight.

Pour the egg mixture into the wok.
Tilt and swirl the wok to spread the
egg to make a thin omelette.

When the omelette is cold enough
to touch, roll it up tightly then cut it
into thin slices.

SALMON WITH CREAMY DILL SAUCE

prep + cook time **25 minutes** serves **4**
nutritional count per serving **48.1g total fat**
(25g saturated fat); 2517kJ (619 cal);
3.2g carbohydrate; 44.6g protein; 0.3g fibre

2 teaspoons olive oil
**4 x 220g (7-ounce) salmon fillets, with the
skin still on**
**1 small brown onion (80g), peeled and
chopped finely**
1 cup (250ml) pouring cream
1 tablespoon coarsely chopped fresh dill

1 Put the oil in a large frying pan. Turn the stove on to medium-low heat and heat the pan. Place the salmon, skin-side down, into the pan; cook for about 5 minutes or until the skin is crisp and golden. Use tongs to turn the salmon over; cook for about 3 minutes or until the fish is cooked the way you like it. Lift the salmon out of the pan. Put it on a large plate; cover with foil to keep it warm.
2 While the fish is cooking, put the onion and cream in a small saucepan. Turn the stove on to medium heat and heat the cream mixture until it is boiling. Turn down the heat and let it simmer, without a lid, for 8 minutes or until it has become thickened slightly. Take the pan off the heat and stir in the dill.
3 Serve the salmon with the creamy dill sauce.

tips **For information about how to peel and chop onion
see page 4.**
**This recipe goes well with steamed green beans and
creamy mashed potato or a simple mixed leaf salad.**

Cook the salmon, skin-side down, until the skin is crisp, then turn the fish over and cook the other side.

When the cream sauce has thickened slightly, remove the pan from the heat and stir in the dill.

SANG CHOY BOW

prep + cook time **40 minutes** serves **4**
nutritional count per serving **11.5g total fat**
(3.6g saturated fat); 1112kJ (266 cal);
8.9g carbohydrate; 29.3g protein; 4.1g fibre

2 teaspoons sesame oil
1 small brown onion (80g), peeled and
    chopped finely
2 cloves garlic, crushed
2cm (¾-inch) piece fresh ginger (10g),
    peeled and grated
500g (1 pound) minced (ground) pork
2 tablespoons water
125g (4 ounces) fresh shiitake mushrooms,
    chopped finely
2 tablespoons light soy sauce
2 tablespoons oyster sauce
1 tablespoon lime juice
2 cups (160g) bean sprouts
4 green onions (scallions), sliced thinly
¼ cup coarsely chopped fresh coriander
    (cilantro)
12 large iceberg lettuce leaves, with white
    parts cut off

1 Put the oil in a wok. Turn the stove on to medium-high heat and heat the wok. Add the brown onion, garlic and ginger; use a wooden spoon to stir-fry until the onion is soft. Add the pork; stir-fry until the pork is browned, breaking up any large lumps with the back of the spoon.
2 Add the water, mushrooms, soy sauce, oyster sauce and lime juice; stir-fry until the mushrooms are tender. Take the wok off the heat. Stir in the bean sprouts, green onion and coriander.
3 Arrange the lettuce leaves on a large platter. Spoon equal amounts of the pork mixture into the lettuce leaf "cups".

tips For information about how to peel and chop onion and crush garlic see page 4.
For information about how to separate lettuce leaves see page 5.
The trick to becoming a stir-fry pro, is making sure you have all the ingredients measured, weighed, peeled, chopped and ready-to-go before you begin frying. Chefs call this "mise en place" which means "everything in its place".

To grate ginger, run the peeled ginger across a microplane (above) or the smallest holes of a grater.

Before you start stir-frying, make sure you have all the ingredients measured, weighed and chopped.

Stir-fry the pork mixture until the pork is browned, breaking up any large lumps with the back of a spoon.

LEMON PANNA COTTA POTS

prep + cook time **15 minutes (+ cooling & refrigeration)**
serves **8**
nutritional count per serving **46.5g total fat
(30.6g saturated fat); 2182kJ (522 cal);
24.7g carbohydrate; 3.1g protein; 0g fibre**

**1 litre (4 cups) thickened (heavy) cream
¾ cup (165g) caster (superfine) sugar
½ teaspoon vanilla extract
3 teaspoons powdered gelatine
1 teaspoon finely grated lemon rind
2 tablespoons lemon juice**

1 Pour the cream into a medium saucepan; add the sugar and vanilla extract. Turn the stove on to low heat and stir the cream mixture with a wooden spoon until it is warm. Sprinkle the gelatine over the cream mixture; stir until the gelatine has dissolved. Don't let the mixture boil.
2 Pour the cream mixture through a fine sieve into a large heatproof jug. Stir in the lemon rind and juice. Leave the mixture to cool.
3 Pour the mixture into eight ⅔-cup (160ml) teacups or plastic dariole moulds; place them on a tray and cover with plastic wrap. Put the tray in the fridge for 4 hours or overnight.
4 Serve the lemon panna cotta in the teacups.

tips **Panna cotta means "cooked cream" in Italian. They are light, custard-like desserts made by simmering cream and sugar together, adding gelatine and then refrigerating until set. They are best served chilled. Panna cotta may also be turned out of their moulds onto a plate for serving.**
serving idea **Serve with fresh raspberries.**

Pour the cream mixture through a fine sieve into a large heatproof jug.

Pour the cooled cream mixture into the eight moulds or teacups.

finn

APPLE BERRY CRUMBLES

prep + cook time **50 minutes** serves **4**
nutritional count per serving **9.3g total fat**
(3g saturated fat); 803kJ (192 cal);
22.3g carbohydrate; 3.1g protein; 3.1g fibre

2 medium apples (300g)
¾ cup (115g) frozen mixed berries
2 tablespoons lemon juice
2 tablespoons light brown sugar
2 tablespoons plain (all-purpose) flour
¼ cup (20g) rolled oats
20g (¾ ounce) butter
¼ cup (30g) finely chopped roasted hazelnuts

1 Turn on the oven to 200°C/400°F and let it
heat up. Spray four ¾-cup (180ml) ovenproof
dishes with cooking oil and place them on an
oven tray.
2 Peel the apples and cut out the cores; chop
the apples coarsely. Put the apple, berries, lemon
juice and half the sugar in a medium bowl; mix
them together with a wooden spoon. Spoon
the fruit mixture into the ovenproof dishes.

3 Put the rest of the sugar in a small bowl
with the flour and oats. Use clean fingertips
to rub the butter into the flour mixture. Stir in
the hazelnuts. Spoon the crumble mixture over
the fruit mixture; use the back of a spoon to
press it down firmly.
4 Put the oven tray with the four dishes into
the oven and bake for about 30 minutes or
until the crumble is light brown.

tips We used a mixture of frozen berries – blueberries,
raspberries, redcurrants and blackberries. You can use
any combination of fresh or frozen berries.
If you don't like hazelnuts you can use the same amount
of macadamia nuts, walnuts or peanuts. Or, to save time
chopping, use crushed peanuts.
serving idea Serve crumbles with a spoonful of yogurt
and a light sprinkling of icing sugar.

Peel the apples and cut out the
cores. Cut the apples into chunks.

Rub the butter into flour and oat
mixture using clean fingertips – the
mixture should look crumbly.

Spoon the apple berry mixture into
four dishes. Spoon crumble mixture
over the top and press down firmly.

FRUIT SKEWERS WITH HONEY YOGURT

prep time **35 minutes** serves 8
nutritional count per serving **2.1g total fat**
(1g saturated fat); 669kJ (160 cal);
28.9g carbohydrate; 6.6g protein; 4g fibre

250g (8 ounces) strawberries
½ medium pineapple (625g)
2 star fruit (320g)
¼ watermelon (1.5kg)
½ small rockmelon (650g)
½ small honeydew melon (650g)
2 cups (560g) yogurt
2 tablespoons honey

1 Cut the green tops from the strawberries.
Peel the pineapple; cut out the hard core then
cut the pineapple into chunks. Cut the star fruit
into thick slices.
2 Cut the watermelon into thick slices. Use a
5cm (2-inch) flower-shaped cutter to cut flowers
from the watermelon flesh.
3 Use a melon baller to scoop balls out of the
rockmelon and honeydew melon.
4 Put the yogurt and honey in a small bowl;
mix them together with a small spoon.
5 Thread the fruits, one type at a time, onto
eight long wooden skewers. Serve the fruit
skewers with honey yogurt.

tip **These skewers can be made a day ahead. Peel and
chop all the fruit, cover with plastic wrap and keep in the
fridge. Thread fruit onto the skewers just before serving.**

Sit pineapple flat on the board (trim
the base if necessary). Run a knife
down the side to cut away the peel.

Cut the pineapple in half, then cut
in half again. Cut out the hard core.
(Only half the pineapple is used.)

Push the melon baller into the flesh
of the melons. Twist the baller to
scoop out balls of melon.

CHOCOLATE-DIPPED FRUIT PIECES

prep + cook time **15 minutes (+ standing)** makes **36**
nutritional count per banana piece **1.7g total fat
(1g saturated fat); 196kJ (47 cal); 7.3g carbohydrate;
0.7g protein; 0.5g fibre**
nutritional count per strawberry **1.7g total fat
(1g saturated fat); 134kJ (32 cal); 3.4g carbohydrate;
0.7g protein; 0.5g fibre**
nutritional count per apricot piece **1.7g total fat
(1g saturated fat); 226kJ (54 cal); 8.4g carbohydrate;
0.9g protein; 1.2g fibre**

**1¼ cups (185g) milk chocolate melts
2 medium bananas (400g), peeled and cut
into 12 thick slices
12 strawberries (250g)
12 dried apricots (150g)**

1 Line a large tray with baking paper.
2 Put the chocolate into a medium heatproof
bowl; place it on top of a medium saucepan of
simmering water on the stove on low heat (don't
let the water touch the base of the bowl). Stir the
chocolate with a metal spoon until it is smooth
and melted. Lift the bowl off the saucepan; place
it on a heatproof mat on the bench.
3 Use tongs to dip each piece of fruit into the
chocolate to cover about half of each piece.
Place the fruit on the tray; leave them until the
chocolate has set.

tips Fruit tastes best when it is dipped in chocolate
on the day you're going to serve it.
You can melt the chocolate in the microwave. Put
the chocolate in a microwave-safe bowl and leave it
uncovered. Put the bowl in the microwave and heat
it on **MEDIUM (55%)** for 1 minute. Stir the chocolate
with a metal spoon. If it hasn't melted completely,
repeat the microwave method, in shorter bursts, until
the chocolate is smooth.

Don't let the water touch the
base of the bowl when melting
the chocolate, or it will overheat
and turn into a thick, grainy lump.

Use tongs to dip the fruit pieces,
one at a time, into the chocolate
then place them onto a tray lined
with baking paper until set.

CARROT AND ORANGE CUPCAKES

prep + cook time **1 hour** (+ cooling) makes **12**
nutritional count per cupcake **14.9g total fat**
(2.8g saturated); 1538kJ (368 cal);
56.4g carbohydrate; 3.6g protein; 1.3g fibre

⅔ cup (160ml) vegetable oil
¾ cup (165g) firmly packed light brown sugar
2 eggs
1 teaspoon finely grated orange rind
1½ cups (210g) firmly packed coarsely
    grated carrot
1¾ cups (260g) self-raising flour
¼ teaspoon bicarbonate of soda
    (baking soda)
1 teaspoon mixed spice
orange glacé icing
2 cups (320g) icing (confectioners') sugar
20g (¾ ounce) butter, melted
2 tablespoons orange juice, approximately

1 Turn on the oven to 180°C/350°F and let it
heat up. Put 12 paper cases into a 12-hole
(⅓-cup/80ml) muffin pan.
2 Put the oil, sugar, eggs and orange rind in
a small bowl; beat with an electric mixer until
the mixture is thick and creamy. Transfer the
mixture to a large bowl. Add the carrot; stir it
into the mixture with a wooden spoon.

3 Sift the flour, bicarbonate of soda and mixed
spice into the bowl; stir until all the ingredients
are mixed together. Spoon the mixture into the
paper cases.
4 Put the pan into the oven and bake for about
30 minutes. Take the pan out of the oven; leave
it for 5 minutes. Carefully turn the cakes out of
the pan; stand cupcakes, top-side up, on a wire
rack to cool.
5 Meanwhile, make the orange glacé icing (see
recipe below).
6 When the cakes are cool, spread the icing
over the tops with the back of a spoon or a
metal spatula. Allow to set before serving.
orange glacé icing Sift the icing sugar into a
small heatproof bowl. Stir in the melted butter
and enough orange juice to make a firm paste
(start with a little and add more if you need to).
Meanwhile, half-fill a small saucepan with water.
Turn the stove on to high and boil the water.
Turn down the heat and let the water simmer.
Put the bowl of icing mixture on top of the
saucepan; stir the mixture until it is soft enough
to spread.

tip **You need about two medium carrots to get enough**
grated carrot for this recipe.

Spoon the mixture evenly into the
paper cases in the muffin pan.

Stir the butter and enough of the
orange juice into the icing sugar
to make a firm paste.

Put the bowl of icing mixture over a
saucepan of simmering water. Stir
until the icing is spreadable.

COCONUT ICE CUPCAKES

prep + cook time **1 hour (+ cooling)** makes **18**
nutritional count per cupcake **8.4g total fat**
(5.9g saturated fat); 669kJ (160 cal);
19.9g carbohydrate; 1.7g protein; 0.8g fibre

60g (2 ounces) butter, softened
½ teaspoon coconut extract
½ cup (110g) caster (superfine) sugar
1 egg
¾ cup (110g) self-raising flour
¼ cup (20g) desiccated coconut
½ cup (120g) sour cream
2 tablespoons milk
coconut ice frosting
1 cup (160g) icing (confectioners') sugar
⅔ cup (50g) desiccated coconut
1 egg white, beaten lightly
pink food colouring

1 Turn on the oven to 180°C/350°F and let it
heat up. Put paper cases into a total of 18 holes
of two 12-hole (2-tablespoons/40ml) deep
flat-based patty pans.
2 Put the butter, coconut extract, sugar and
egg in a small bowl; beat with an electric mixer
until the mixture is light and fluffy. Use a flour
sifter to sift half the flour into the bowl. Add half
the coconut, half the sour cream and half the
milk; stir them in with a wooden spoon. Sift the

rest of the flour into the bowl, then stir in the rest
of the coconut, sour cream and milk. Spoon
the mixture into the patty cases.
3 Put the patty pans into the oven and bake
for about 20 minutes. Take the pans out of the
oven and leave for 5 minutes. Carefully turn the
cupcakes out of the pans; stand cupcakes,
top-side up, on wire racks to cool.
4 Meanwhile, make the coconut ice frosting
(see recipe below).
5 Drop small spoonfuls of frosting – first white
and then pink – onto the cakes; spread them
over the cakes with a hot, wet palette knife.
coconut ice frosting Use a flour sifter to sift
the icing sugar into a small bowl. Add the
coconut and egg white; mix well. Put half the
mixture into another small bowl; add a few
drops of pink food colouring and mix it in.
Leave the other bowl white.

tip Use a hot wet palette knife to spread the frosting
over the cakes. Either run your palette knife under the
hot water tap or stand it in a cup of hot water. A small
butter knife could also be used to spread the icing.

Spoon the cake mixture into the
paper cases in the patty pans.

Stir a few drops of pink colouring
into one of the bowls of frosting.
Leave the other bowl white.

Use a hot wet palette knife to
spread the pink and white coconut
frosting over the cupcakes.

MUESLI SLICE

prep + cook time **40 minutes** makes **30 pieces**
nutritional count per piece **6.4g total fat**
(3.3g saturated fat); 460kJ (110 cal);
11.3g carbohydrate; 1.6g protein; 1.4g fibre

125g (4 ounces) butter, chopped
⅓ cup (75g) firmly packed light brown sugar
2 tablespoons honey
1⅓ cups (120g) rolled oats
½ cup (40g) shredded coconut
½ cup (75g) self-raising flour
½ cup (65g) dried cranberries
½ cup (80g) finely chopped dried pineapple
½ cup (70g) slivered almonds
2 tablespoons pepitas

1 Turn on the oven to 180°C/350°F and let it heat up. Spray a 20cm x 30cm (8-inch x 12-inch) rectangular pan with cooking oil; use baking paper to line the base and long sides, leaving 5cm (2-inch) of paper hanging over the edges of the pan.

2 Put the butter, sugar and honey in a medium saucepan. Turn the stove on to low heat and stir the mixture with a wooden spoon until the sugar has dissolved. Stir in the rest of the ingredients.

3 Spoon the mixture into the pan; press it down firmly with the back of a wooden spoon. Put the pan in the oven and bake for about 20 minutes. Take the pan out of the oven and leave it to cool. Cut the slice into 30 pieces.

tips **You can buy pepitas (dried pumpkin seeds) and dried pineapple at health-food stores and most supermarkets. If you can't find dried pineapple, use the same amount of finely chopped dried apricot instead.**

Line the base and long sides of the greased pan with baking paper, leaving 5cm (2 inches) over sides.

Press the mixture firmly over the base of the pan with the back of a wooden spoon.

YOGURT, BERRY AND WHITE CHOCOLATE MUFFINS

prep + cook time **40 minutes** makes **12**
nutritional count per muffin **7.2g total fat**
(2.5g saturated fat); 807kJ (193 cal);
25.3g carbohydrate; 5.6g protein; 2.4g fibre

1½ cups (225g) wholemeal self-raising flour
½ cup (110g) caster (superfine) sugar
2 tablespoons vegetable oil
2 eggs, beaten lightly
1 cup (280g) low-fat yogurt
1 cup (150g) frozen mixed berries
100g (3 ounces) white eating chocolate,
**   chopped coarsely**

1 Turn on the oven to 180°C/350°F and let
it heat up. Spray the holes of a 12-hole
(⅓-cup/80ml) muffin pan with cooking oil.
2 Use a flour sifter to sift the flour and sugar
into a large bowl. Add the rest of the ingredients
(make sure the berries are still frozen); stir with
a wooden spoon about 10 times – not too
much, as the batter should be lumpy.
3 Spoon the mixture into the pan holes. Put the
pan in the oven and bake for about 30 minutes.
Take the pan out of the oven and leave for
5 minutes. Carefully turn the muffins out of the
pan; stand muffins, top-side up, on a wire rack
to cool.

tips These muffins are best served warm.
Keeping the berries frozen means their colour doesn't
ooze out into the mixture, turning it blue.
You could also use milk or dark (semi-sweet) chocolate
instead of the white chocolate.
We used low-fat plain yogurt but you can use low-fat
berry-flavoured yogurt, if you like.

Stir the oil, eggs, yogurt, berries and
chocolate into the flour mixture. Do
not overmix, it should be lumpy.

Carefully turn the muffins out of the
pan onto a wire rack, then turn
them top-side up to cool.

BANANA BREAD

prep + cook time **45 minutes (+ cooling)** serves **8**
nutritional count per serving **3.4g total fat**
(1.8g saturated fat); 748kJ (179 cal);
33.2g carbohydrate; 3.7g protein; 1.3g fibre

1¼ cups (185g) self-raising flour
1 teaspoon ground cinnamon
20g (¾ ounce) butter
½ cup (110g) firmly packed light brown sugar
1 egg, beaten lightly
¼ cup (60ml) milk
½ cup mashed banana

1 Turn on the oven to 220°C/425°F and let it heat up. Spray a 14cm x 21cm (5½-inch x 8½-inch) loaf pan with cooking oil; use baking paper to line the base of the pan.
2 Use a flour sifter to sift the flour and cinnamon into a large bowl; use clean fingertips to rub the butter into the flour mixture. Add the sugar, egg, milk and banana; stir with a wooden spoon about 10 times – not too many, as the batter should be lumpy. Use a spatula to spread the mixture evenly into the pan.
3 Put the pan in the oven and bake for about 30 minutes. Take the pan out of the oven and leave it for 5 minutes. Carefully turn the banana bread out of the pan; stand bread, top-side up, on a wire rack to cool.

tips **You need one large overripe banana (230g) for this recipe. Mash the banana in a small bowl with the back of a fork.**
Keep uncut banana bread in an airtight container for up to two days, or freeze it for up to three months.
serving idea **Toast banana bread slices and spread with butter.**

Use clean fingertips to rub the butter into the flour mixture. It should look crumbly.

Spread the mixture evenly into the loaf pan with a rubber spatula.

SLICES also known as
on rashers; made from
ork side, cured and smoked.
AKING PAPER also parchment
paper or baking parchment – a
silicone-coated paper that is
primarily used for lining baking
pans and oven trays so cakes
and biscuits won't stick making
removal easy.

BEANS

mexe-beans (mexican-style
beans) a spiced combination
of kidney or pinto beans,
capsicum and tomato.

sprouts also known as bean
shoots; tender new growths of
assorted beans and seeds
germinated for consumption.
The most readily available are
mung bean, soya beans,
alfalfa and snow pea sprouts.

BICARBONATE OF SODA also
known as baking or carb soda;
a mild alkali used as a leavening
agent in baking.

BREAD

french stick a long, narrow
cylindrical loaf. Has a crisp
brown crust and light chewy
interior. A standard bread stick
is 5-6cm wide and 3-4cm tall,
but can be up to a metre in
length. It is also known as a
baguette or french loaf.

turkish also known as pide;
comes in long (about 45cm)
flat loaves as well as individual
rounds (rolls).

tortillas thin, round unleavened
bread originating in Mexico.
Two kinds are available, one
made from wheat flour and the
other from corn (maize).

BREADCRUMBS, PACKAGED

purchased, fine-textured,
crunchy, white breadcrumbs.

BUTTER 125g is equal to one
stick (4 ounces) of butter.

CABANOSSI a processed
sausage popular in Southern
Europe. Made from pork and
beef and seasoned with
spices and fresh garlic.

CHEESE

bocconcini from the diminutive
of 'boccone' meaning mouthful,
is the term used for a delicate,
semi-soft, white cheese – a
smaller version of mozzarella.
Spoils rapidly so must be kept
under refrigeration, in brine, for
1 or 2 days at most. Smaller
ones are also known as baby
or cherry bocconcini, and are
the size of a cherry.

fetta a crumbly goat- or
sheep-milk cheese with a
sharp salty taste.

parmesan also known as
parmigiano; a hard, grainy
cow's-milk cheese.

CHICKEN SEASONING available in
the spice aisle at supermarkets.

CHIPOLATA SAUSAGES also
known as 'little fingers'; spicy,
coarse-textured beef sausage.

CHOCOLATE

Melts discs of compounded
chocolate ideal for melting
and moulding.

white contains no cocoa solids
but gets its sweet flavour from
cocoa butter. Sensitive to heat
so watch when melting.

CINNAMON dried inner bark of
the shoots of the cinnamon
tree; available in stick (quill) or
ground form.

COCONUT

desiccated unsweetened,
concentrated, dried, finely
shredded coconut.

shredded thin flat strips of
dried coconut.

CORIANDER also known as
cilantro, pak chee or chinese
parsley; a bright-green leafy
herb with a pungent flavour.
Both the stems and roots of
coriander are used; wash well
before using. Also available
ground or as seeds; these
should not be substituted for
fresh coriander as the tastes
are completely different.

CRANBERRIES, DRIED they
have the same slightly sour,
succulent flavour as fresh
cranberries. Available in most
supermarkets.

CREAM we use fresh cream,
also known as pouring, pure or
single cream, unless otherwise
stated. It has no additives.
Minimum fat content 35%.

sour a thick, commercially-
cultured soured cream.
Minimum fat content 35%.

thickened a whipping cream
containing a thickener.
Minimum fat content 35%.

CUCUMBER

lebanese short, slender and
thin-skinned. Probably the
most popular variety because
of its tender, edible skin, tiny
seeds and sweet, fresh taste.

telegraph long and green with
ridges running down its entire
length; also known as
continental cucumber.

DILL also known as dill weed. Has
a sweet anise/celery flavour.

FLAT-LEAF PARSLEY a flat-leaf variety of parsley; also known as continental or italian parsley.

FLOUR

plain an all-purpose flour made from wheat.

self-raising (self-rising) plain or wholemeal flour combined with baking powder in the proportion of 1 cup flour to 2 teaspoons baking powder.

FRENCH-TRIMMED (frenched) a butchers' term referring to a cutting method where excess sinew, gristle and fat from the bone end of meat cutlets, racks or shanks are removed and the bones scraped clean.

GELATINE a thickening agent. Available as a powder, or in sheet form, known as leaf gelatine. Three teaspoons of dried gelatine (8g or one sachet) is roughly equivalent to four gelatine leaves.

GINGER also known as green or root ginger; the thick root of a tropical plant.

HAM HOCKS the lower portion of a pig leg, made up of meat, fat and bone. Generally used to flavour dishes

HAZELNUTS also known as filberts; plump, grape-size, rich, sweet nut. Remove the inedible skin by rubbing heated nuts vigorously in a tea towel.

LETTUCE

butter (boston) have small, round, loosely formed heads with soft, buttery-textured, sweet tasting, leaves. Because the leaves are quite tender, they require gentle washing and handling.

cos also known as romaine lettuce; the traditional Caesar salad lettuce. Baby cos has smaller leaves.

iceberg a heavy, firm, round lettuce with tightly packed leaves and a crisp texture.

MIXED SPICE a blend of ground spices usually consisting of cinnamon, allspice and nutmeg.

MUSHROOMS

button small, cultivated white mushrooms with a delicate, subtle flavour.

shiitake when fresh, are also known as chinese black or forest mushrooms; although cultivated, they have the earthiness and taste of wild mushrooms. Are often used as a substitute for meat in some Asian vegetarian dishes.

MUSTARD

dijon pale brown, distinctively flavoured, fairly mild-tasting french mustard.

wholegrain also known as seeded mustard. A french-style coarse-grain mustard made from crushed mustard seeds and dijon-style french mustard.

OIL

cooking spray we use a cholesterol-free cooking spray made from canola oil.

olive made from ripened olives. Extra virgin and virgin are the best, while extra light or light refers to taste, not fat levels.

peanut pressed from ground peanuts; this is the most commonly used oil in Asian cooking because of its high smoke point (capacity to handle high heat without burning).

sesame made from roasted, crushed white sesame seeds; a flavouring rather than a cooking medium.

vegetable sourced from plants.

OLIVES

black have a richer and more mellow flavour than the green ones, and are softer in texture. Sold either plain or in a piquant marinade.

green are harvested before fully ripened and are, as a rule, denser and more bitter than their black relatives.

ONION

brown and white these are interchangeable, however, white onions have a more pungent flesh.

green also known as scallion or, incorrectly, shallot; an immature onion picked before the bulb has formed. Has a long, bright-green edible stalk.

red also known as spanish, red spanish or bermuda onion; a sweet-flavoured, large, purple-red onion.

OREGANO a herb, also known as wild marjoram; has a woody stalk with clumps of tiny, dark green leaves that have a pungent, peppery flavour. Can be used fresh or dried.

PALETTE KNIFE a knife with a wooden or plastic handle and a thin, flat, dull blade; it can be straight or offset, which has an angle at the join of the handle and the blade. Used a lot when icing cakes.

PEPITAS edible pumpkin seeds with a nutty flavor that have had their white hull removed.

PIZZA BASES pre-packaged for home-made pizzas. They come in a variety of sizes (snack or family) and thicknesses (thin and crispy or thick).

RICE PAPER SHEETS also known as banh trang. Made from rice paste and stamped into rounds. They are quite brittle and will break if dropped; dipped momentarily in water they become pliable wrappers for fried food and uncooked vegetables. They make good spring-roll wrappers.

RICE VERMICELLI NOODLES also known as sen mee, mei fun or bee hoon. Are used throughout Asia in spring rolls and cold salads; similar to bean thread noodles, only longer and made with rice flour instead of mung bean starch.

ROLLED OATS groats (oats that have been husked) that are steamed-softened, flattened with rollers, dried and then packaged for consumption as a cereal product.

SAUCE
fish also called nam pla or nuoc nam; made from pulverised salted fermented fish, most often anchovies. Has a pungent smell and a strong taste, so use sparingly.
oyster Asian in origin, this rich, brown sauce is made from oysters and their brine, cooked with salt and soy sauce, and thickened with starches.
soy made from fermented soya beans. Several variations are available in most supermarkets and Asian food stores.

Light soy is a fairly thin, pale, but salty tasting, sauce; used in dishes where the natural colour of the ingredients is to be maintained. Not to be confused with salt-reduced or low-sodium soy sauces.
tomato pasta made from a blend of tomatoes, herbs and spices.

SHALLOTS also called french shallots, golden shallots or eschalots; small, brown-skinned, elongated members of the onion family. Grows in tight clusters similar to garlic.

SPINACH also known as english spinach and, incorrectly, silver beet. Its thick, soft oval leaves and stems are both edible. Baby spinach is also available.

SPLIT PEAS also known as field peas; a green or yellow pulse (which are the edible seeds of legumes, like lentils, beans, peas and chickpeas) grown especially for drying. They are split in half along a centre seam. Used in soups, stews and, occasionally, spiced and cooked on their own.

STARFRUIT also known as carambola, five-corner fruit or chinese starfruit; is pale green or yellow in colour. Has a clean, crisp texture; flavour may be either sweet or sour, depending on variety and when picked. No need to peel or seed. Are slow to discolour; avoid ones with brown spots or streaks.

SUGAR
brown soft, finely granulated sugar retaining molasses for its colour and flavour.

caster also known as superfine or finely granulated table sugar.
icing also known as powdered or confectioners' sugar; is white granulated sugar crushed together with a small amount of cornflour.

TOMATOES
cherry also known as tiny tim or tom thumb tomatoes; small and round.
egg also called plum or roma; small, oval-shaped tomatoes often used in Italian cooking.
sun-dried tomato pesto a thick paste made from sun-dried tomatoes, oil, vinegar and herbs.
truss vine-ripened tomatoes with the vine still attached.

VANILLA EXTRACT made by pulping chopped vanilla beans with a mixture of alcohol and water. Gives a strong solution, and only a couple of drops are needed to flavour most dishes.

VINEGAR
rice a colourless vinegar made from fermented rice and flavoured with sugar and salt.
white wine made from a blend of white wines.

WOMBOK also known as napa, petsai, peking or chinese cabbage. Elongated in shape with pale green, crinkly leaves; Is the most common cabbage in South-East Asian cooking.

ZUCCHINI (courgette) a small, pale- or dark-green, yellow or white vegetable belonging to the squash family. Harvested when young, its edible flowers can be stuffed then deep-fried or oven-baked.

CONVERSION CHART

MEASURES

One Australian metric measuring cup holds approximately 250ml, one Australian metric tablespoon holds 20ml, one Australian metric teaspoon holds 5ml.

The difference between one country's measuring cups and another's is within a 2- or 3-teaspoon variance, and will not affect your cooking results. North America, New Zealand and the United Kingdom use a 15ml tablespoon. All cup and spoon measurements are level. The most accurate way of measuring dry ingredients is to weigh them. When measuring liquids, use a clear glass or plastic jug with metric markings.

We use large eggs with an average weight of 60g.

DRY MEASURES

METRIC	IMPERIAL
15g	½oz
30g	1oz
60g	2oz
90g	3oz
125g	4oz (¼lb)
155g	5oz
185g	6oz
220g	7oz
250g	8oz (½lb)
280g	9oz
315g	10oz
345g	11oz
375g	12oz (¾lb)
410g	13oz
440g	14oz
470g	15oz
500g	16oz (1lb)
750g	24oz (1½lb)
1kg	32oz (2lb)

LIQUID MEASURES

METRIC	IMPERIAL
30ml	1 fluid oz
60ml	2 fluid oz
100ml	3 fluid oz
125ml	4 fluid oz
150ml	5 fluid oz
190ml	6 fluid oz
250ml	8 fluid oz
300ml	10 fluid oz
500ml	16 fluid oz
600ml	20 fluid oz
1000ml (1 litre)	1¾ pints

LENGTH MEASURES

METRIC	IMPERIAL
3mm	⅛in
6mm	¼in
1cm	½in
2cm	¾in
2.5cm	1in
5cm	2in
6cm	2½in
8cm	3in
10cm	4in
13cm	5in
15cm	6in
18cm	7in
20cm	8in
23cm	9in
25cm	10in
28cm	11in
30cm	12in (1ft)

OVEN TEMPERATURES

These oven temperatures are only a guide for conventional ovens.
For fan-forced ovens, check the manufacturer's manual.

	°C (CELSIUS)	°F (FAHRENHEIT)
Very slow	120	250
Slow	150	275-300
Moderately slow	160	325
Moderate	180	350-375
Moderately hot	200	400
Hot	220	425-450
Very hot	240	475

The imperial measurements used in these recipes are approximate only. Measurements for cake pans are approximate only. Using same-shaped cake pans of a similar size should not affect the outcome of your baking. We measure the inside top of the cake pan to determine sizes.

GENERAL INDEX

how to
avocado, seeding 16
bacon, draining cooked 36
bread, slicing 36
bruschetta, preparing 19
cake
  lining rectangular pan 68
  turn out a cooked cake 5
capsicum, peel and coring 39
chocolate
  dipping fruit 63
  melting 63
citrus rind, grating 5
crumble, making 59
eggs
  boiling 7
  frying 8
  omelettes for fried rice 51
  poaching 27
  separating 4
frittata
  preparing pan 23
  removing from pan 23
garlic, peeling and crushing 4
ginger, grating 55
icing
  preparing glacé 64
  preparing two-toned 67
lettuce, separate leaves 5
meat
  crumbing lamb racks 44
  rolling meatballs 47
  shredding ham hocks 31
  slicing beef 40
  stir-frying 55
melon, making balls 60
nuts, browning 40
onion, peeling and
  chopping 4

orange (see also citrus rind)
  peel and segment 11
pasties, preparing 45
pineapple, peeling 60
pizza, cutting rounds from
  large base 20
potato
  preparing for chips 32
  preparing baked shells 35
quesadillas, preparing 24
rice paper rolls, filling and
  rolling 12
rice, preparing for fried rice 51
salmon, cooking 52
sandwiches, preparing 15, 16
stir-frying
  cooking meat 55
  preparing vegetables 55
tomato
  seeding 24, 32
  quarter 39
zucchini, grating 20

RECIPE INDEX

A
apple berry crumbles 59

B
bacon
  and corn creamed stuffed
    potatoes 35
  and potato soup 28
  frittatas, bacon, tomato and
    fetta 23
banana bread 72
bean and coriander
  quesadillas 24
beef salad, vietnamese 40
berry apple crumbles 59

berry, yogurt and white
  chocolate muffins 71
blt salad 36
boiled egg with toast soldiers
  7
bread, banana 72
breakfast, cooked english 8
bruschetta fingers 19

C
cabanossi pizzas, mini 20
cakes
  carrot and orange cupcakes
    64
  coconut ice cupcakes 67
  yogurt, berry and white
    chocolate muffins 71
carbonara with peas,
  spaghetti 43
carrot and orange cupcakes
  64
chicken
  and vegetable pasties 48
  fried rice 51
  mayo, celery and walnut
    sandwiches 15
chocolate
  dipped fruit pieces 63
  white chocolate yogurt and
    berry muffins 71
club sandwich 16
coconut ice cupcakes 67
cooked english breakfast 8
creamed corn and bacon
  stuffed potatoes 35
crumbles, apple berry 59
cupcakes
  carrot and orange 64
  coconut ice 67

INDEX

D

drink, passionfruit sparkler 11

E

egg
  boiled with toast soldiers 7
  english breakfast, cooked 8
  spinach, ham and poached
    egg on toast 27
  tomato, fetta and bacon
    frittatas 23

F

fried rice, chicken 51
frittatas, tomato, fetta and
  bacon 23
fruit
  pieces, chocolate-dipped 63
  skewers with honey yogurt
    60

G

greek salad 39
guacamole with potato
  wedges 32

H

ham
  and pea soup 31
  poached egg and spinach
    on toast 27
herb-crumbed lamb racks 44
honey yogurt with fruit
  skewers 60

L

lamb racks, herb-crumbed 44
lemon panna cotta pots 56

M

meatballs napoletana 47
mini cabanossi pizzas 20
muesli slice 68
muffins, yogurt, berry and
  white chocolate 71

N

noodle and vegetable rice
  paper rolls 12

O

orange and carrot cupcakes
  64

P

passionfruit sparkler 11
pasta
  spaghetti carbonara with
    peas 43
pasties, chicken and
  vegetable 48
pea and ham soup 31
pizzas, mini cabanossi 20
pork
  meatballs napoletana 47
  sang choy bow 55
potato
  and bacon soup 28
  creamed corn and bacon
    stuffed 35
  wedges with guacamole 32

Q

quesadillas, bean and
  coriander 24

R

rice paper rolls, noodle and
  vegetable 12
rice, chicken fried 51
rolls, rice paper, noodle and
  vegetable 12

S

salad
  blt 36
  greek 39
  vietnamese beef 40
salmon with creamy dill
  sauce 52

sandwich
  bean and coriander
    quesadillas 24
  bruschetta fingers 19
  chicken, mayo, celery and
    walnut 15
  club 16
sang choy bow 55
seafood, salmon with creamy
  dill sauce 52
skewers, fruit, with honey
  yogurt 60
slice, muesli 68
soup
  bacon and potato 28
  pea and ham 31
spaghetti carbonara with peas
  43
spinach, ham and poached
  egg on toast 27

T

tomato, fetta and bacon
  frittatas 23

V

vegetable
  and chicken pasties 48
  and noodle rice paper rolls
    12
vietnamese beef salad 40

W

white chocolate yogurt, berry
  and muffins 71

Y

yogurt, berry and white
  chocolate muffins 71

If you like this cookbook, you'll love these...

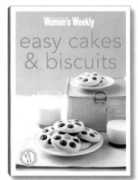
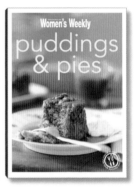